HIGH-SPEED KNIFE FIGHTING

Highland Knife Fighting
With the Dirk and Sgian

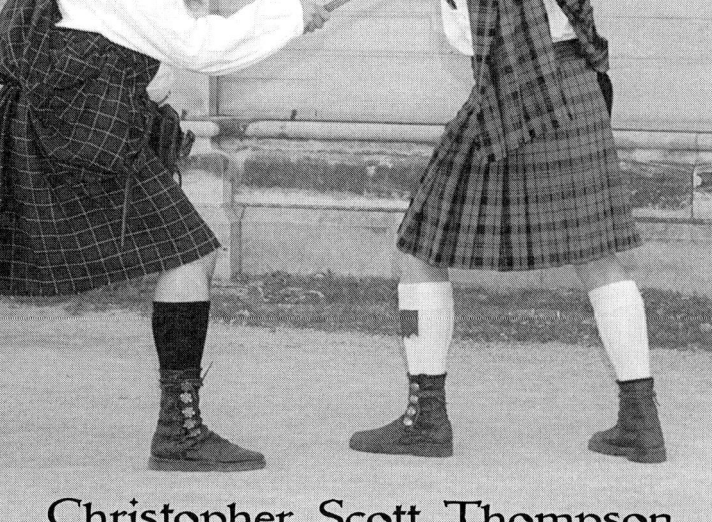

Christopher Scott Thompson
with Louie Pastore

Paladin Press ~ Boulder, Colorado

Other books by Christopher Thompson:
Highland Martial Culture

Highland Knife Fighting: With the Dirk and Sgian
by Christopher Scott Thompson
(with additional contributions by Louie Pastore)

Copyright © 2007 by Christopher Scott Thompson

ISBN 13: 978-1-58160-566-2
Printed in the United States of America

Published by Paladin Press, a division of
Paladin Enterprises, Inc.
P.O. Box 1307
Boulder, Colorado 80301 USA
+1.303.443.7250

Direct inquiries and/or orders to the above address.

PALADIN, PALADIN PRESS, and the "horse head" design are trademarks belonging to Paladin Enterprises and registered in United States Patent and Trademark Office.

All rights reserved. Except for use in a review, no portion of this book may be reproduced, stored in or introduced into a retrieval system, or transmitted in any form without the express written permission of the publisher. The scanning, uploading and distribution of this book by the Internet or any other means without the permission of the publisher is illegal and punishable by law. Please respect the author's rights and do not participate in the any form of electronic piracy of copyrighted material.

Neither the author nor the publisher assumes any responsibility for the use or misuse of information contained in this book.

Visit our website at www.paladin-press.com.

Contact the author at one of the following Web sites:
www.noctiviganti.com or www.cateransociety.com

Suas leis a' Ghàidhlig!

WARNING

Training with knives is inherently dangerous. Use caution and practice only with appropriate protective gear and aluminum or wood training knives. Take care not to injure yourself, your training partner, or anyone else. The information in this book is presented *for academic study only*.

Table of Contents

1. The Dirk in Gaelic Society 1

2. Mastering the Dirk 5
    Holding the Dirk
    Carrying the Dirk
    Using the Dirk with the Sword and Targe
    Throwing the Dirk

3. Guards 15
    First Guard
    Second Guard
    Third Guard
    Fourth Guard
    Fifth Guard

4. Responding to an Attack 21
    Time
    Distance
    Footwork
    Using Your Hands
    Quickdraw
    Sudden Attacks

5. Throws from Highland Wrestling 39
The Back Heel
Sweeping or Tripping
Hamming
The Crook
Hankering the Heel
The Lock
The Buttock
The Swinging Hipe
The Chip
Shifting

6. Bone-Breakings 47
Headbutting
Palm Strike Displacement
Trapping and Controlling
Kicking
Punching

7. Knife Against Knife 53
On the Defensive
On the Offensive

8. Going on the Offensive 57
Displacing Counterattacks Using the Free Hand
The Attack
The Feint
The Invitation
The Continuation
The Recovery or Throwing of the Opponent

9. The Dirk Dance Positions 65

TABLE OF CONTENTS • ix •

10. Exercises and Drills **71**
    Stabbing and Slashing Exercises
    The Twelve Doors of the Soul Exercise
    The "Leslie" Exercise
    Two-Person Drills
    Advanced Quickdraw Drill

Appendix 1 .... **95**
    Combative Techniques in the Scottish Dirk Dance

Appendix 2 .... **105**
    The Manx Dirk Dance

Appendix 3 .... **107**
    The Cateran Society

Glossary **109**

About the Authors **111**

ACKNOWLEDGMENTS

Thanks to Bob Giordano, Ian Graham, and Bill Pooler for helping me prepare the initial sketches that served as models for the photographs in this book. Thanks also to Alastair McIntyre for permission to quote from Electric Scotland's collection of Highland history and literature; to Dr. Michael Newton for his support, ideas, and the use of his extensive library; and to *A Heart's Desire Photography* and the members of the Wolves of Dunvegan, who assisted with the photographs: Phread Cichowski, Daniel Sorensen, Bryan Hunt, and Curtis Judd.

The weapons pictured in this book are from the collection of Phread Cichowski and include three antique dirks from the 18th century or earlier.

DISCLAIMER

This book is not intended to teach the use of the knife for self-defense in a modern context. The Gaelic world in the clan period was a knife culture—in other words, a society in which people habitually carried knives and used them not only for daily tasks, but also to avenge insults and wage clan feuds. The Gaelic dirk is far longer than most modern blades. Also, the legal and ethical context of contemporary knife combat is different from that of the old Gaelic world.

The author does not claim to have experience with actual knife combat but simply to have researched historic Gaelic knife use from the available sources.

For information on the modern use of the knife, a good place to start is Marc MacYoung's *Knives, Knife Fighting, and Related Hassles* from Paladin Press. MacYoung's approach is straightforward and realistic, and addresses many issues of modern knife use—issues that no one who carries a blade can afford to ignore.

A Note about Sources

Within the past 50 years, British Army veterans in Scotland practiced a type of dirk fencing in which the dirk was held point up in a stance similar to the low medium guard of the regimental broadsword style, with attacks directed to the opponent's fingers and leading wrist. Scottish backhold coach Willie Baxter described this style to Cateran Society researcher Louie Pastore, who has since done further research on this method.[1]

It is not known whether this is a survival of an older style of dirk combat, a method used by commandos in World War II (some of whom carried dirks), or simply a martial sport. In any case, it is a style in which both fencers have their dirks in hand at the beginning of the bout. Gaelic accounts of dirk use suggest that this would rarely have been the case in the clan period.[2] Other sources suggest that the dirk was often used with the

---

1. See the Cateran Society discussion group archives at http://sports.groups.yahoo.com/group/cateran/
2. See the accounts of dirk use included in this book.

point down, in a stance resembling sword and targe combat rather than a modern fencing style of footwork.[3]

Furthermore, while 19th-century dirks have hilts that are long enough to make the forward grip convenient, older dirks generally do not. Every pre-1800 dirk I examined featured a very small hilt that would have favored the reverse grip.[4] Archibald MacGregor's *Art of Defence* (1791) states, "When they came to close quarters, they directed it, as you see me do at present, sometimes to the right, left, front, or rear, according to the place where the enemy was."[5] Such a method is only possible with the reverse grip.

This book describes the use of the dirk in the context of clan feuds and sudden ambushes. Louie Pastore may explore, in a future volume, the style of dirk fighting described by Baxter.

The grips and stances described herein were taken from the description of dirk combat in James Logan's *The Scottish Gael* (1833), the Scottish dirk dance recorded by the Fletts, Archibald MacGregor's *Art of Defence* from 1791, and the positions shown for Highland broadsword combat in the Penicuik sketches.

The use of the free hand was based on the methods of the Highland Officer's *Anti-Pugilism* text. The targeting was derived from the medieval Gaelic medical manuscript known as the *Judgments of Diancecht*. The kicking, foot-sweeps, and throws were drawn from the Scottish dirk dance and traditional

---

3. J.F. and T.M. Flett, *Traditional Step-Dancing in Scotland* (Scottish Cultural Press, 1996), 178: "In battle a dirk would have been clasped in the fist, with the point down in order to be used in a slashing movement upwards or in a jabbing movement downwards." Also see *The Scottish Gael* by James Logan, 1833, which describes dirk combat, and *Drawn After the Quicke*, a 16th-century German woodcut of Gaelic warriors showing a long knife being used in the reverse grip with passing footwork.

4. The dirks examined were from the collection of Cateran Society member Phread Cichowski.

5. Paul Wagner and Mark Rector, *Highland Broadsword: Five Manuals of Scottish Regimental Swordsmanship* (Chivalry Bookshelf, 2004): 133–134.

Highland wrestling. Other close-distance techniques were based on streetfighting attacks still used in modern Scotland. The footwork was based on the Highland broadsword exercise and on older fencing manuals describing the use of passing steps.

This is my own attempt at a speculative reconstruction of early dirk combat through synthesizing a number of fragmentary sources. As such, it should not be considered definitive.

Christopher S. Thompson
January 2007

The Dirk in Gaelic Society

I n Japanese martial culture, the sword is often described as "the soul of the samurai," and a mystical reverence is associated with that weapon. The samurai wore a short sword or a dagger indoors and in other situations where the long sword would not have been appropriate. This short sword or dagger therefore served as the last line of defense in case of a surprise attack.

In Scots Gaelic martial culture, the dirk played a very similar role. The most solemn and binding oaths were sworn on the dirk, and when the Highlanders were disarmed following Culloden, they considered the ban on the dirk the most objectionable of all. However, the dirk's use was not restricted to combat, as it was also a convenient tool for quartering deer, cutting firewood, and so forth.

A number of accounts in Scottish history and oral tradition show the role of the dirk in Gaelic society and the circumstances in which it was most likely to be used. It was seen as almost sacred, capable of slaying even supernatural creatures, such as hags and giants.

• 2 • HIGHLAND KNIFE FIGHTING

The loss of the boy angered the witch and in her madness she began killing the agents of McDonald of Islay as they crossed over by ferry. In desperation, someone approached a Buie of Largiebreac and promised him a nearby farm if he would kill her. The Buie's son stepped forward and presently he was locked in mortal combat with the Cailleach. With her supernatural powers, the witch brought the son to his knees and triumphantly exclaimed, "Thou art in extremity, a' Mhic Mheadh Buidhe." Yet, the youth, gathering strength from his ancestors, returned, "My grandmother, who is on the hither side of Alba, is here and will come to help me if I be." With these words, young Buie raised his dirk and plunged it into the Cailleach's evil heart, killing her instantly.[1]

An oath sworn on the dirk was considered to be absolutely binding.

After cautioning them not to mention the meeting to any one, he swore them to secrecy upon his naked dirk, and then dismissed them. They kept their word.[2]

The Camerons, living at issue with the government, had many disorderly men among them, and tascal-money became accordingly with them a peculiar abomination. To so great a height did this run, that a large portion of the clan voluntarily took oath to each other, over a drawn dirk, according to their custom, that they would never receive any such reward; otherwise might the weapon be employed in depriving them of their lives.[3]

....

1. From the "Buie Clan History" at electricscotland.com/webclans/atoc/buie2.htm.
2. From the "General History of the Highlands: Prince Charles Edward Stuart," as found at electricscotland.com/history/charles/89.htm.
3. Robert Chalmers, "Domestic Annals of Scotland from the Reformation to the Revolution," 1874, as found at electricscotland.com/history/domestic/vol3ch4f.htm.

THE DIRK IN GAELIC SOCIETY • 3 •

Although worn by all classes of society, the dirk was frequently the primary weapon of the common clansmen, who could not always afford to carry broadswords. It was essentially a symbol of one's manhood and status as a valued member of the community, and for men full adulthood carried with it the right to wear the dirk and the bonnet.

The dirk was also worn indoors, while the broadsword generally was not. As such, it was the favored weapon for acts of revenge, which, again as in Japanese society, were not always expected to conform to any principles of fair play. (Traditional rules about hospitality were important, but as the Glencoe massacre and other incidents show, not everyone could be relied on to uphold these rules.)

Because of its use indoors and in sudden attacks, much emphasis was placed on quickdraw skills with the dirk. As Logan says, "(I)t could be drawn in an instant, and this was of some importance in the event of a sudden assault, or so close a contention as would prevent a free use of the sword," as would generally have been the case in the cramped space of Highland dwellings.[4]

As it says in Burt's "Letters": "(I)t is a concealed mischief, hid under the plaid, ready for secret stabbing, and in a close encounter there is no defense against it."[5]

---

4. James Logan, *The Scottish Gael*, 1833, p. 216.
5. Ibid.

Mastering the Dirk

The dirk (*biodag* in Gaelic) is a long knife, often made from a cut-down sword blade. Most experts believe it to be descended from the medieval ballock dagger. There is no guard for the hand, and the blade is sharp on the true edge only, though the first inch or so of the false edge might also be sharpened. The handle is often decorated with Celtic-style knotwork designs.

The dirk is quite long. A custom-made dirk should extend to your elbow when held in the standard ("reverse") grip.[1] Many surviving examples are 20 inches or even a bit longer.

HOLDING THE DIRK

The dirk is usually held with the point down and the true edge facing out. In modern knife fighting, this is often called the "reverse" or "ice pick" grip. Your fingers should wrap securely around the handle, while your thumb provides extra control,

....

1. J.F. and T.M. Flett, *Traditional Step-Dancing in Scotland* (Scottish Cultural Press, 1996): 178.

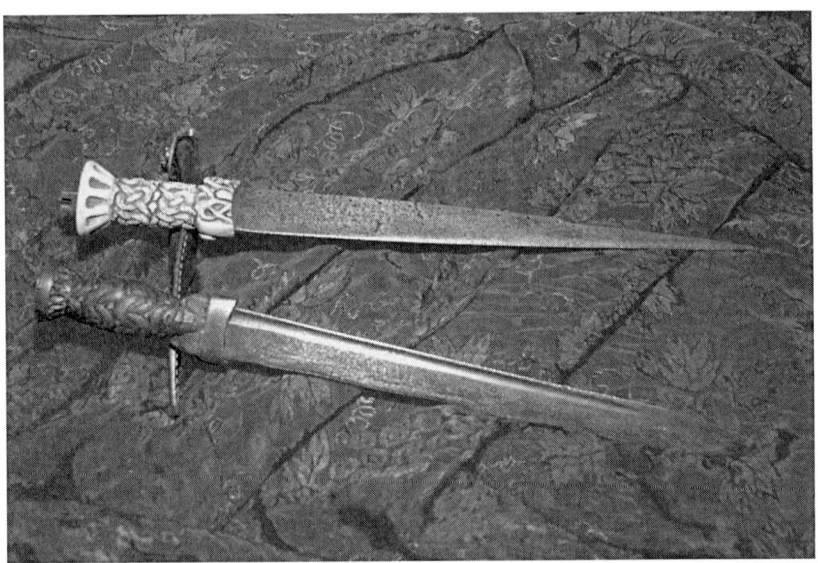

Antique fighting dirks from the collection of Phread Cichowski.

This dirk was made from the blade of a Drury backsword, as can be seen by comparing the "GR Drury" mark with that on the Drury backsword shown here.

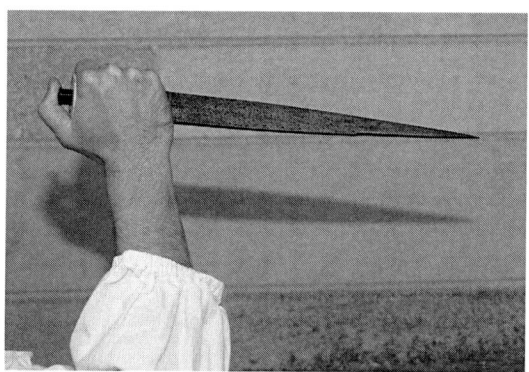

The reverse grip.

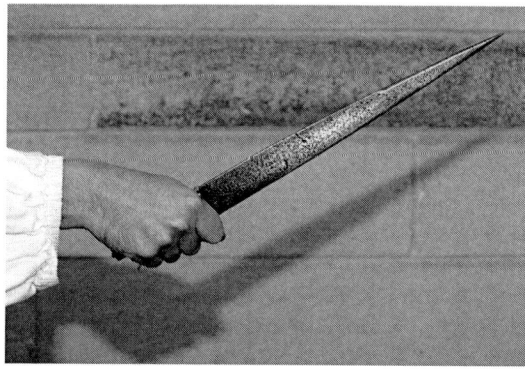

The forward grip.

either held against the handle firmly or resting on top.

Some situations call for the use of the forward, or sword, grip, in which the dirk is held with the point forward, as you would hold a broadsword. In this grip, the thumb can be on the back of the hilt (in which case it is often called the sabre grip) or wrapped around the handle securely.

In the reverse grip, keeping the thumb on the top will help keep your hand from sliding down onto the blade during a strong thrust. In the forward grip, keeping the thumb on the back of the hilt provides improved edge control but less stability in your hand.

It is important to be able to shift between the reverse and forward grips quickly and smoothly. You should practice doing so with your training weapon until you can shift from one grip to the other with ease.

Today a number of excellent dirk replicas are commercially available, but, unfortunately, most of the time the sheath is designed in such a way that the dirk can only be drawn with the edge facing inward. In this case, there is no option but to turn the edge so that it faces outward as soon as the blade clears the sheath.

CARRYING THE DIRK

If you can't get to your weapon when you need it, then you're not really carrying it in the first place. There are several effective ways to carry the knife—and a few that are not so effective.

Hanging from Your Strong Side

This was one of the two most common ways to carry the dirk. The *sgian* (Gaelic for a knife of any type) could also be carried this way if you were not carrying a dirk. From this position, it's easy to raise your hand and draw the knife in the reverse grip, simultaneously raising your free hand to ward off the approach of any attacker and stepping out of distance or off-line as needed.[2]

The strong-side carry.

Hanging Between Your Legs

Although this seems like an odd way to carry a knife, it is shown in many contemporary pictures of Highland warriors.

....

2. The dirk is carried this way in a German woodcut of Mackay's Highlanders from 1631 and in an illustration of Black Watch soldiers in 1746 that can be found on page 70 of Antony MacKenzie Smith's *Glenshee: Glen of the Fairies* (Tuckwell Press, 2000).

Carrying the dirk between the legs.

This position allows for a very fast draw, and although it looks as if it would be uncomfortable to sit down with your dirk hanging this way, it actually isn't. The weapon can easily be adjusted so that it rests in a horizontal position while you're sitting, which would also allow you to draw it under a table without being noticed, as long as you do so slowly and evenly so there is no sound.[3]

Concealed in the Plaid

Because men usually wore dirks openly, a man whose weapon was not visible must have been viewed with suspicion. Concealing a second dirk in the folds of your plaid could allow you to get closer to your target.[4]

Under the Armpit

The modern *sgian dubh* (dress knife) has its origin in the *sgian achlais* (armpit knife). The knife can be drawn very quickly from

....

3. The dirk is carried this way in every plate of George Grant's *New Highland Military Discipline of 1757*.
4. Burt describes the dirk as being concealed in the plaid in his "Letters," quoted by Logan in *The Scottish Gael*.

The armpit knife.

this position, but you must raise your free hand as you draw to prevent your opponent from rushing you.[5]

In the Shirtsleeves

Some warriors actually carried a sgian in each shirtsleeve, just in case they were somehow deprived of the broadsword, targe, bow, musket, pistols, dirk, and various other weapons that they usually carried.[6] We don't know exactly how the knife was held in place, but for it to be of any use it would have had to be easily accessible. If you carry a sgian in the shirtsleeve of your free arm, you can raise your arm into its usual defensive position in front of the body while you draw the blade with your strong hand

....

5. From scottish-swords.com: "The *sgian-achlais* (oxter-knife) or *sgian dubh* (black knife) was a secret weapon, hidden somewhere between the clothing, often underneath the arm-pit."
6. Smith, *Glenshee*, p. 40.

MASTERING THE DIRK • 11 •

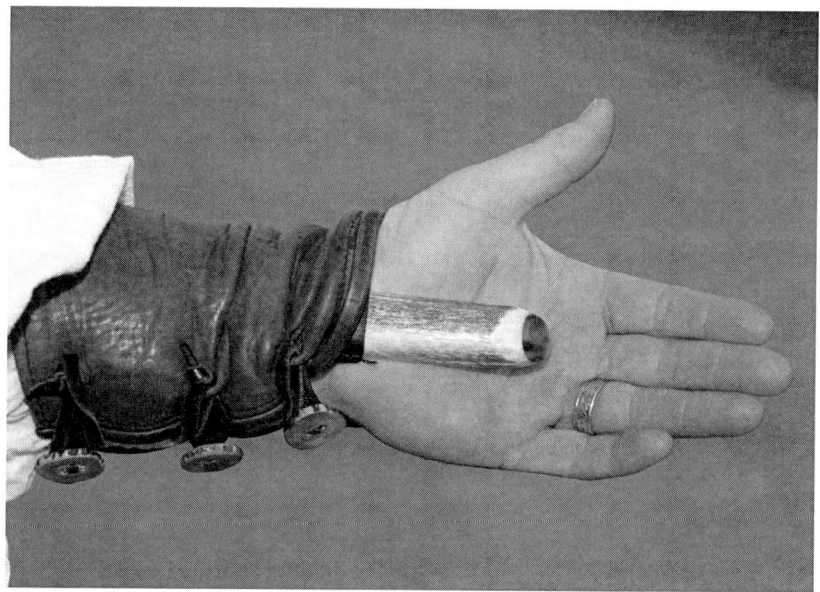

A knife concealed in the shirtsleeve.

simultaneously. Your free arm will ward off or at least slow down any attacker as you draw the weapon, although of course you should combine the draw with evasive footwork, such as the shift or the traverse. (Refer to the section on footwork in Chapter 4 for more information.)

In the Sock or Boot

This is how the sgian dubh is usually worn with formal Highland dress, but it has little combat value. You won't get much of a chance to reach into your sock in a combat situation.

Hanging from Your Weak Side

Some pictures do show Highlanders carrying the dirk on their left sides, although these could be left-handed warriors. Carrying your knife on your weak side is not a very good idea in general, because your opponent can rush in and pin your arm in place as you attempt to draw your weapon.

USING THE DIRK WITH THE SWORD AND TARGE

Highland warriors often fought with a broadsword in one hand and both a targe and dirk in the other. If you are fighting this way, hold the dirk held point down, with the sharp edge facing out. The point will protrude a short distance beyond the rim of your targe. Because the rim of the targe can be used as a punching weapon on its own, the following techniques are performed in exactly the same way regardless of whether you have a dirk. For complete instructions on the use of the sword and targe, see Thomas Page's *Use of the Broadsword* (1746) or seek instruction from the Cateran Society.

One of the most basic attacks with the targe is to punch the rim into your enemy's face. If your targe is held high and you are close enough to strike your enemy this way, you perform the attack by extending your arm crisply, as if stabbing downward with a knife. If you have a dirk and targe, the dirk will stab him in the face while the targe rim breaks his teeth and drives him backward. You can perform the same attack if your targe is held low, by extending the arm forward and up into his face. In this case, if you have a dirk its tip will also cut his face on the way up.

If you can take control of your opponent's sword with your own sword (especially if his sword arm is extended), you can strike his sword arm with your dirk and targe in much the same way. In certain positions, you may be able to perform a targe strike against his shoulder.

If your targe is temporarily in front of you with the flat facing the enemy (as it would be after a parry on your sword side), you can strike the enemy with the face of your targe or with its spike (if it has one).

You should immediately follow up any targe and dirk attack with a sword attack to finish the combat.

THROWING THE DIRK

According to Archibald MacGregor in 1791, the dirk was also used as a throwing knife:

> *It was also used much in the same manner as a lance: for I have been informed of those people were dextrous marksmen with it; for they would throw at a considerable distance, and hit the object to a certainty.*[7]

While the specific method used for throwing the dirk has not survived, knife throwing is a skill that can be learned through repetition, even without formal instruction. Using a high-quality dirk reproduction, simply throw the weapon at a target (such as a figure of a man showing the Twelve Doors of the Soul; see page 71 for more information) until you can hit your target consistently. This type of training requires special care, as a thrown dirk is obviously very dangerous. Most knife throwing experts use only specially weighted knives for the purpose, so not all dirks will be equally effective.

....

7. Paul Wagner and Mark Rector, *Highland Broadsword: Five Manuals of Scottish Regimental Swordsmanship* (Chivalry Bookshelf, 2004): 134.

Guards

There are four engaging guards with the dirk or sgian (first, second, fourth, and fifth guards), and one intermediary position, which is the third guard.

The first guard.

FIRST GUARD

To take this guard, step forward with your left foot (if you are right-handed) 1 1/2 foot lengths, and pivot your right foot to 45 degrees. You can step up on the ball of your rear foot if you wish. Hold the dirk beside your head about the level of your temple, with the point down and aimed at your enemy, and the true edge facing outward. Hold your left hand loosely beside your head as if it were a targe, or at your waist or in front of your body at the level of the breast, with your hand loose and your palm facing inward. Hold the free hand this way for all the guards.[1]

---

1. This is the most natural guard, as the dirk is drawn from its sheath. It is shown in the 16th-century German woodcut *Drawn After the Quicke*.

The second guard.

SECOND GUARD

To take this guard, lower the dirk until it is beside your right hip, with the point facing behind you, in the reverse grip. In this position, the opponent should not be able to see your weapon.[2]

....

2. In *The Scottish Gael* (pp. 216–217), Logan describes dirk combat, stating that the dirk was held in the reverse grip and aimed in four directions. He was probably basing this information on MacGregor's *Lecture on the Art of Defence* (1791), in which MacGregor stated: "When they came to close quarters, they directed it, as you see me do at present, sometimes to the right, left, front, or rear, according to the place where the enemy was." This guard is based on the statements of Logan and MacGregor to the effect that the dirk was sometimes directed "to the rear."

The third guard.

THIRD GUARD

Immediately after slashing at your enemy from the second guard, the dirk will sometimes be in front of your chest with the point facing the enemy. It is possible to stab the enemy immediately from this position, without returning to one of the engaging guards first.[3]

....

3. This intermediary position is depicted in *Robbing the Eagle's Nest*, a print by R.R. McIan in *Highlanders at Home* by James Logan and R.R. McIan, 1845.

The fourth guard.

FOURTH GUARD

This guard is much like the St. George guard of the regimental broadsword system. Change to the forward grip and raise the dirk above your head so that the point is to your left (if you are right-handed) and the true edge is facing up, with the blade parallel to the ground. This guard is probably ineffective with a shorter knife, but because the dirk is as long as a short sword, it can make powerful cuts from this position. It can also be used to help throw the opponent. (Throws are discussed in more detail on pages 39–46.)[4]

....

4. This guard is derived from the Scottish dirk dance, as described on page 179 of the Fletts' *Traditional Step-Dancing in Scotland*: "Flourish the dirk up across the front of the face to a position just above and slightly in front of the head with the back of the hand uppermost."

The fifth guard.

FIFTH GUARD

To take this guard, lower the dirk until it is beside your right hip, with the point aimed in front of you, in the forward grip. In this position, the opponent should not be able to see your weapon. You can also take this guard with the right foot forward, using the dirk somewhat as you would use a sword, but in that case you must be especially on guard against attacks to your hand or arm.[5]

You should practice changing from guard to guard until you can do so fluidly and easily.

....

5. This guard is also derived from the Fletts' description of the dirk dance.

Responding to an Attack

I f you are attacked with a knife, there are two factors that will determine what your options are and what is likely to happen. These factors are time and distance.

TIME

The worst-case scenario is when an opponent is close enough to strike you and his weapon is already drawn, while yours is still in the sheath. Most of the things you could do to defend yourself would take you longer than the time your assailant needs to complete the attack. There are things you can do even in such a bad situation, but for now it's simply important to realize that everything depends on time. Vigilance will help buy you time, because the sooner you realize what's happening, the more time and options you will have.

Once an attack begins, you will want either to take the attacker down immediately even though you are unarmed, or buy yourself enough time to escape or draw your own blade.

In modern society, escape would be by far the best choice, because it offers the best chance of survival and the fewest legal and ethical problems. However, this would not always have been the case in the old Gaelic society, because any act that was perceived as cowardly would cause you to lose face, or *cliu*. Therefore ,we will assume that your goal is to either defeat the attack unarmed or buy enough time to draw your own weapon. Remember that this mentality is geared toward the warrior society of the old Highlands and not necessarily to modern survival.

DISTANCE

Distance is closely connected to time. If an attacker has to step forward before he can reach you, you have more options than if he were already in range. There are three types of distance, which are the same as those found in broadsword fencing.

- Out of distance: You cannot reach your opponent with a single step forward.
- In distance: You can reach your opponent with a single step forward.
- Close distance: You can reach your opponent without stepping forward.

Remember that your distance may not be the same as your opponent's distance. If he is taller than you, he may be able to strike you even while you are not in distance to strike him. If you shift out of distance of his attack, you may still be in distance to strike his head or arm.[1]

FOOTWORK

Whatever type of attack you face, you will need to use footwork effectively. Your use of footwork will depend on something

---

1. For a discussion of distance in broadsword fencing, see *Lannaireachd: Gaelic Swordsmanship* by Christopher Thompson.

"READY FOR SECRET STABBING"

Obviously an assassin is not going to give you fair play—his goal is to get close to you without arousing your suspicion and stab you when you cannot defend yourself. If an enemy can get close enough to strike you while your own weapon is still sheathed, your chances of survival are remote. Therefore, the most important defense against a knife attack is vigilance. This isn't something you can think about only when you are training—if you aren't vigilant all the time, it will be useless. Vigilance is a combination of awareness and strategic behavior.

First, don't make yourself an easy target. When you're in public, avoid sitting or standing in a way that limits your ability to move or to see what's going on around you. Don't expose your back to the crowd if you can help it. Don't allow people to get too close to you or to stand at an angle where they can easily attack you. You must be aware of the physical space around you and all the people in it, and move through that space in such a way that gives you the advantage in any physical conflict. This is something you can only learn by thinking about it habitually whenever you are in public. Take note of anyone you consider likely to be dangerous, and be especially careful not to let such people position themselves so they can attack you. Don't lose track of where these people are.

Because dirks were ordinarily worn in plain view on the hip, anyone whose dirk could not be seen would be considered a threat. Even if you can see someone's weapon, however, that doesn't always mean you are safe. A second weapon could be concealed, ready for use.

A man with folded arms or with his hands behind his back or with a hand out of sight behind his leg or held in an awkward way could be concealing a knife.[2]

---

2. Marc "Animal" MacYoung, *Knives, Knife Fighting and Related Hassles* (Paladin Press 1990): 43–53 and 71–72.

called the line, which is an imaginary line running between you and your opponent. No matter where the two of you are positioned, the line runs straight between the two of you. All your footwork will happen in relation to this line.

You can move either straight forward or straight back along the line, but you can also move at an angle to the line—to the right forward, the left forward, straight right, straight left, back right, and back left.

When the opponent attacks you, he will be moving toward you using one of the following types of footwork, which are the same steps used in sword practice.

- **Pass:** The rear foot takes a full step forward, passing the front foot, which pivots to assume the rear foot position. This is much like an ordinary walking step.
- **Step in:** The front foot takes a large step forward, but the rear foot doesn't immediately follow.
- **Advance:** The front foot steps forward, followed by the rear foot.

Any of these steps can be taken on the line or at an angle to the line. In response, your first priority is to control the distance. To do this, you can move into the attack or move away from it. It is possible to move in successfully against a knife attack, but this is very dangerous and requires a higher level of skill than is needed to move away.

You may be forced to move in if there is an obstacle behind you and you are unable to retreat, or you may choose to do so deliberately if you believe you can control the opponent. If you do so, you will advance, pass forward, or step in, and then use the close-distance fighting skills described herein.

Avoiding an attack with footwork is called slipping the attack. To slip the attack by moving out of distance, you can retreat, leap back, pass back, traverse, or shift. Once again, this footwork is essentially the same as that of the sword exercise.

- **Retreat:** Your rear foot steps back, followed by your front foot.
- **Leap back:** You leap back with both feet out of the range of the attack.
- **Pass back:** Your front foot takes a full step backward, passing by your rear foot.
- **Shift:** Your front foot darts back till it is almost even with your rear foot.
- **Traverse:** A traverse is any step that takes you off the line. You can traverse by simply stepping to the right or left, or to the right reverse or left reverse, or you can combine the traverse with other maneuvers. For example, you can pass back while pivoting off-line, carrying your entire body away from the attack and off the line.

You must practice your footwork until you can carry out any of these actions smoothly, quickly, and with perfect balance. Losing your balance in a knife fight would probably be fatal.

When slipping an attack, you want to be out of distance and off-line, in that order of priority. Moving out of distance buys you time, but if your attacker keeps moving forward you quickly lose this advantage. A man moving forward is always faster than a man moving backward. For this reason, you should regain the initiative by counterattacking at the same moment you move out of distance, or make sure to move off the line as well and then follow up with another tactic.[3]

USING YOUR HANDS

Whether you are moving into the attack or away from it, you must be using your hands at the same time. The hand holding

---

3. If you are not an experienced broadsword fencer, you should seek training in footwork from a historical fencing instructor.

your knife is called your knife hand, while the other hand is your free hand.

When using your hands to defend against a knife, you will likely be cut on the hand or arm. Taking a cut on your free arm is much less dangerous than being cut or stabbed on your body or on your knife arm. A glancing blow against your free arm will not necessarily stop you from continuing the fight, as long as it doesn't cut the vulnerable inside of the arm.

For this reason, you should keep the inside of your free hand and arm facing your body, using the outside for all your defensive actions. Only turn the inside of your hand toward your opponent when you need to get a grip on his body or to push the flat of his blade away in some circumstances.[4]

As you are stepping in or out in response to your opponent's attack, raise your free hand to prevent the opponent from rushing in and to deflect the attack or grip the opponent's knife arm if possible. The free hand should move away from your body in a semicircle, smacking the attack away from you. Ideally, you want your wrist to make contact with his wrist, but even if you strike the flat of his blade, you will not be cut. As your wrist strikes his wrist, you can turn your hand to get a grip on his knife arm if you get the chance. The key point to remember is to deflect the attack *away* from your body. Don't push it in front of you.

To know best how to use your free hand, you must understand the four zones of the body.

Just as with the broadsword, the dirk has an inside and an outside. If you stand in position and hold the dirk out in front of you like a broadsword, you can see this most easily. If you are a right-handed person, everything to the left of the dirk is the inside line, and everything to the right of the dirk is the outside line. However, you will also have to deal with left-handed fighters, so you should not think in terms of left side and right side, but rather of inside and outside. In this context,

....

4. MacYoung, *Knives, Knife Fighting, and Related Hassles,* p. 67.

RESPONDING TO AN ATTACK • 27 •

Deflecting up and to your left.

Deflecting down and to your left.

Deflecting up and to your right.

Deflecting down and to your right.

"line" refers to a zone and is not the same as the line between you and your opponent.

Most attacks with the knife will come from the outside to the inside, so to gain an advantage in positioning you will want to maneuver yourself toward your opponent's outside, where it will be more difficult for him to strike you. The fourth guard, however, can easily strike in a much wider arc, so an opponent in this guard may be able to strike you even if you are far to his outside.

The inside and outside lines are further subdivided into high and low, so that we have the four zones: outside high, inside high, outside low, and inside low, exactly as in broadsword fencing.

Most (but not all) knife attacks from a right-hander will target your inside lines, so you will usually need to deflect either inside high or inside low. In other words, if you are also a right-hander, you will use your free hand to deflect up and to your left or down and to your left, always moving the arm in a semicircle and deflecting away from your body with the outside of your arm.

Occasionally, you'll need to deflect outside high (up and to your right) or outside low (down and to your right).

If you slip the attack and are out of distance, you won't need to deflect it with your hand. In this case, your hand should come up in a ready position as you are slipping the attack. There are three ready positions for the free hand.

1. Loosely beside your head with the palm facing inward[5]
2. In front of your body at the level of the breast, with your hand loose and your palm facing inward[6]
3. At your waist[7]

....

5. As shown in Donald McBane's *Expert Sword-Man's Companion of 1728*.
6. As shown in the Highland Officer's instructions for the hanging guard in *Anti-Pugilism*.
7. As shown in the *Drawn After the Quicke* woodcut.

Positions of the free hand.

You can use whichever position you prefer. Bringing your free hand to a ready position will allow you to deflect a second attack by an opponent who keeps charging in after his initial attack has been slipped. This will you give you more time to get your own weapon into play.

QUICKDRAW

Despite its exalted status in Gaelic culture, the dirk was used primarily for sudden quarrels and killings.

> When encamped at Collace, Montrose gave an entertainment to his officers, on returning from which Ardvoirlich, "heated with drink, began to blame Kilpont for the part he had taken in preventing his obtaining redress, and reflecting

RESPONDING TO AN ATTACK • 31 •

against Montrose for not allowing . . . what he considered proper reparation. Kilpont, of course, defended the conduct of himself and his relative, Montrose, till their argument came to high words, and finally, from the state they were both in, by an easy transition, to blows, when Ardvoirlich, with his dirk, struck Kilpont dead on the spot."[8]

The dirk was also useful in prosecuting blood feuds through surprise attacks.

All went well till the moment for the murderous attack by the Comyns was all but reached, when Mackintosh suddenly took the initiative, and gave his own signal, whereupon each Mackintosh at the board drew his dirk and stabbed the Comyn next him to the heart.[9]

As you can see from these excerpts, the victims of a dirk attack rarely had any opportunity to draw their own weapons. In the case described above, even though the Comyns had actually planned a surprise attack of their own, they were still unable to

---

8. "General History of the Highlands," electricscotland.com/history/genhist/hist43.html, drawn from the *History of the Scottish Highlands, Highland Clans and Scottish Regiments,* mostly compiled around 1830 with some updates done in the late 1870s. Edited by John S. Keltie, F.S.A. (Scot).

9. From the MacKintosh clan history, electricscotland.com/webclans/m/mackint2.html.

draw their knives in time when the Mackintoshes beat them to the punch. This seems to have bred a certain degree of paranoia among those whose lifestyles made them likely targets for attack.

> *Ewen, although well stricken in years, is still strong and healthy, and his muscular frame gives promise of a protracted age. The dangers to which his irregular mode of life exposes him, require his utmost vigilance, and frequently his greatest physical exertion. To prevent surprise, he has always a loaded gun close to his bed by night, and his dirk by his side during day.*[10]
>
> *On one occasion he was pointed out to a person anxious to see a character so noted, by the incautious observation, "there he is," on which Ewen drew his dirk, and in the confusion which arose, MacKenzie, the stranger, was wounded.*[11]
>
> *MacLachlan instantly fled, and was obliged to wander through the Highlands and isles for many years, in constant dread of being captured or slain by his enemies. During this time it was his practice to sleep in caves, or the least accessible mountains, and even when in the shelter of a house, he always rested his head on his naked dirk, a weapon peculiarly convenient in case of sudden or close attack.*[12]

The skill of quickdraw seems to have survived even into the 20th century, as in this account of a Highland piper from World War I.

> *Once in a pub after a parade, he was tossing back his Black & White scotch, and an ornery drunk started on him—the usual—"Hey! Guys in skirts! What are you? Sissies?" etc. Donald ignored the lout until he reached for his Cameron Officers' dirk.*

....

10. "McIan's Highlanders at Home: Mac Phee, the Outlaw," electricscotland.com/history/home/chapter20.htm.
11. Ibid.
12. From the MacLachlan clan history, electricscotland.com/webclans/m/maclach2.html.

RESPONDING TO AN ATTACK • 33 •

Faster than you would believe, it was out of its sheath and quivering in the top of the bar! Donald growled, without even looking at the idiot, "Touch it again and you'll be wearing it!"[13]

As you can see, a fast draw was an essential survival skill with the dirk. At the same time you are slipping the attack and defending with your free hand, you also must be drawing your knife. If you are not wearing a dirk on your hip, you will have to go for the sgian under your armpit or in your shirtsleeve. If you have to draw a knife from your shirtsleeve, the act of putting your free arm in the ready position will also put your knife close enough to be drawn quickly.

In theory, however, you would always have a knife at your side. Despite its great length, the dirk can be drawn with incredible speed. This is because the blade is relatively narrow and perfectly straight and the sheath is designed like a sword scabbard for an easy draw. Even without practice, the dirk will seem to leap into your hand. However, it is important to practice your quickdraw skills to be sure you can bring your weapon into play in 1 second at most.

To practice your draw, stand with your dirk at your side and imagine a sudden attack. Slip the attack as described above, while raising your free hand to a ready position. At the same time, wrap your knife hand around the dirk hilt with your knuckles facing forward and your thumb on top. Draw the dirk smoothly from its sheath into a position from which you can strike. This is the first guard, the most typical guard of the dirk.

Sheath your dirk, lower your arms, and repeat the process. You will have to practice quickdraw constantly to develop your skill.

One useful quickdraw drill is to do 10 repetitions each of a variety of possible scenarios, including the following.

---

13. Jim Taylor, "Mini Biographies of Scots and Scots Descendants: Leslie, Donald Rory," electricscotland.com/webclans/minibios/l/leslie_donald.htm.

- Slip to the right and back while deflecting up and to the left with your free hand and drawing your dirk with your knife hand.
- Slip straight to the right while deflecting up and to the left with your free hand and drawing your dirk with your knife hand.
- Slip forward and to the right while deflecting up and to the left with your free hand and drawing your dirk with your knife hand.
- Repeat the above while deflecting down and to your left.
- Repeat the above while deflecting up and to your right and slipping to your left.
- Repeat the above while deflecting down and to your right and slipping to your left.
- Practice turning, deflecting, and drawing against an opponent approaching rapidly from behind.

For safety reasons, use only training knives for these drills, not sharp dirks.

SUDDEN ATTACKS

In general, your first response to a sudden knife attack will be as follows:

1. Get out of distance and, if possible, off-line.
2. Deflect with your free hand or raise it to a ready position.
3. Draw your own weapon.

These actions will occur simultaneously, but getting out of the way of the attack is the most important aspect. Now we will look at how distance and time affect this general plan.

Attacks from Out of Distance

In this scenario, someone who is standing out of distance from you either draws his knife in a threatening gesture or comes charging in at you with his knife drawn.

If he draws his knife in a threatening way but is not yet trying to use it or to close the distance, you have all the time you need to draw your own dirk. An opponent who shows his weapon in this way might back down if you draw your own weapon with intent to use it. The knife is a deadly weapon, and the choice to draw it in a conflict is a life or death decision. Never draw your own weapon merely to intimidate. Against a serious opponent, this attempt reveals your lack of resolve.

If the attacker is making a committed rush at you while your knife is sheathed, he will close the distance between you rapidly. Therefore, you must increase the distance between the two of you using the footwork described herein. This will buy you enough time to regain the initiative.

The plan in this situation is very simple in theory.

1. Control the distance and get off the line of the attack. For example, you can take a large step toward your back right, removing you from the line and increasing the distance.
2. Raise your free hand to a ready position.
3. Draw your own weapon.

If you cannot buy yourself enough time to draw your weapon by the time the attacker has closed the distance, you will have to deflect his attack and use close-distance fighting techniques as described herein. Attacks from out of distance are the easiest to deal with and are usually the result of a moment of a rage. However, a calculated knife attack will be made from the closest distance the attacker can manage.

Attacks from In Distance

In this scenario, the attack comes from close enough that the attacker can reach you with a single step. In this case, you may have to deflect his attack with your free hand as previously described. If there is no time to draw your own weapon, you may also have to close the distance deliberately and use the tech-

An attack from out of distance.

niques described herein for close-distance fighting. However, if you don't immediately choose to close the distance, the basic plan is still very simple.

1. Control the distance and get off the line of the attack. For example, you can shift to make sure his initial attack falls short and then turn that maneuver into a pivot, removing your body from the line and increasing the distance.
2. Use your free arm to deflect his attack, smacking it away from your body in a semicircular motion using the outside of the arm and deflecting in whatever direction is appropriate (depending on whether he is attacking your outside high, inside high, outside low, or inside low). If you succeed in slipping the attack completely with your footwork so that you do not need to deflect with your free hand, then immediately

An attack from in distance.

be ready to deflect his follow-up attack. If possible, grab his knife arm to immobilize it.
3. Draw your own weapon or close in and use the close-distance fighting techniques described herein.

Attacks from Close Distance

This is the worst-case scenario, in which you are attacked from close distance while your weapon is still sheathed. It is also the most likely scenario, in that a determined enemy will certainly do everything he can to get close to you before launching his attack. In this situation, you will use techniques derived from traditional Highland wrestling, the dirk dance, and similar sources. The dirk dance makes use of eight foot positions, which are similar but not identical to those ordinarily used in Highland dancing and which are also similar to the traditional methods of Highland wrestling. These positions will be introduced one by one as the various techniques are described. Each of these techniques should be practiced carefully with a training partner and a safe training weapon. The techniques should be practiced very slowly at first to allow the unarmed person to perform the counter.

Note that the dirk dance foot positions are numbered differently here than in the original sources. This is done because the original sources use the terminology of Highland dancing, which is likely to be confusing to someone who is not a dancer.

If you are lucky enough to spot the attacker at the moment he puts his hand on his knife to draw it, you can close the distance rapidly and pin his knife hand in place with your free hand. At the same time, you can reach across his body to get a grip with your knife hand and throw him with one of the techniques described herein. Otherwise, you will have to displace his attack with your free hand and catch and immobilize his knife arm if you can—at least for long enough to make the throw.

Throws from Highland Wrestling

Rather than attempting to draw one's own dirk in response to a surprise attack, a better solution was often to meet the attack empty-handed, trusting to one's skill in Highland wrestling.

> *The contest became such betwixt them, that the servant drew his dirk to rid him of the youth's trouble, which the other wrung out of his hands, and downright killed him with it.*[1]
>
> *A discomfited competitor for the honor, giving way to vindictive and furious passion, went to the class meeting armed with a dirk, and endeavored to fix a quarrel on young Manly. Failing in this, and more exasperated by a coolness that his violent words could not disturb, he rushed upon him and endeavored to plunge the deadly weapon into his breast. The blow was warded off, and*

---

1. Robert Chalmers, "Domestic Annals of Scotland from the Reformation to the Revolution," 1874, electricscotland.com/history/domestic/vol1ch6.htm.

before the assailant knew what was going on, he was disarmed; and then, it is said, a fitting chastisement was inflicted.[2]

On the battlefield, skill in wrestling went hand in hand with the use of the dirk in close combat.

Cobham's regiment, which had just returned from foreign service, however, stood its ground for some time, and breaking through the first line of the Highlanders, trampled many of them under foot. A singular combat then ensued. Deprived of the use of their broadswords, some of the Highlanders, who lay stretched on the ground, had recourse to their dirks, which they plunged into the bellies of the horses. Others seized the riders by their clothes, and dragging them from their horses, stabbed them with the same weapon.

In this melée the chief of Clanranald made a narrow escape, having been trodden down, and before he was able to rise a horse fell dead upon him, the weight of which prevented him from extricating himself without assistance. While in this perilous situation, he saw a dismounted dragoon and a Highlander struggling near him, and for a time the issue seemed doubtful. The anxiety of the chief, whose own preservation seemed to depend on the success of this clansman, was soon relieved, when he saw the Highlander throw his antagonist, and instantly despatched him with his dirk.[3]

The essence of dirk combat seems to have been found in vigilance, a fast draw, and skill at wrestling. Following are some throws from traditional Highland backhold wrestling.

....

2. Carol Hardy Bryan, "Basil Manly II, Distinguished Baptist Leader, Had Important Ties to Edgefield," quoting from a book about the Manly family, electricscotland.com/familytree/newsletters/quill/mar2003.htm.

3. "General History of the Highlands: Prince Charles Edward Stuart," electricscotland.com/history/charles/53.htm.

THROWS FROM HIGHLAND WRESTLING

THE BACK HEEL

The attacker passes straight forward, stabbing down at you. Step to your forward left to get to his outside, while deflecting his attack with your free hand and getting a grip on his knife arm. At the same time, use your knife hand to get a grip on his jacket or shirt. Get your foot behind his and use your heel to push his heel forward rapidly and forcefully, while pushing your weight against him in the opposite direction so that he falls on his back. Try not to fall with him, but if you do, make sure that you're on top and that you retain control of his knife hand. The position of your foot as you perform the back heel is similar to the first foot position of the dirk dance.

SWEEPING OR TRIPPING

This is virtually the same technique as the back heel, except that instead of targeting the attacker's heel for the takedown, you target the side of his foot on the outside. This time, you catch his knife hand and get a grip on his shirt or jacket with your knife hand, while sweeping his foot out from under him with a sudden kick. You must target his stationary foot as he steps forward with his other foot, and you must do so from the outside in a position similar to the second or eighth positions of the dirk dance.

HAMMING

This is a variation on the back heel technique. In this case, you get your foot behind the attacker's knee (on his inside or outside) and use your heel to push his knee forward rapidly and forcefully, while pushing your weight against him in the opposite direction so that he falls on his back. In this case, your foot will be in a position similar to the fourth position of the dirk dance.

THE CROOK

In this case, you catch or deflect the attacker's knife arm while stepping forward and to his inside. To perform the crook,

Throwing the attacker.

THROWS FROM HIGHLAND WRESTLING • 43 •

Hamming.

wind your foot around his leg and use it as a lever to overbalance him either forward (the fore crook) or backward (the back crook). Your right arm should be placed across his body, pushing against his left shoulder, to push him backward, or you can push him from behind to throw him forward across your foot.

HANKERING THE HEEL

This is a technique for an opponent whom you cannot immediately throw. After you have a grip on him, get your foot behind his and unbalance him slowly with constant pressure from your heel against his, while pushing your weight against him in the opposite direction so that he falls on his back. Make sure you maintain control of his knife arm as you are grappling with him.

THE LOCK

In this case, the attacker is holding his knife in the less-common forward grip. He passes forward, stabbing straight at you. Step forward, placing your leg between your attacker's legs. At the same moment, deflect his attack with your free hand and get a grip on his knife arm, while gripping his shirt or jacket with your free hand. Twist your forward leg around his leg (his right leg if you're using your left leg, and vice versa), so that your foot wraps completely around his leg, with your toes by his shin. Turn forcefully to the side (the left side if you are using the left leg, and the right side if you are using the right leg) to throw him backward. Do not lean forward too far, or the opponent may throw you forward. In this case, your foot will be in a position similar to the third position of the dirk dance.

THE BUTTOCK

This throw is easier to perform if your hold is relatively loose. It is usually performed with the left hip, but either hip

THROWS FROM HIGHLAND WRESTLING • 45 •

may be used. After stepping in and getting a grip, twist your body so that your hip is beneath your opponent's belly. Then twist forcefully to the opposite side, lifting him off the ground in a turning motion, so that he falls underneath you. To perform the cross buttock, do the same as just described, but with your body twisted so that your back is almost to the opponent, with your leg across and in front of his leg. If you are performing the throw with your left hip, your leg is across his right leg, and vice versa.

THE SWINGING HIPE

After establishing your grip, lift your opponent rapidly off the ground and swing him to one side while pushing the inside of his thigh in the other direction with your knee, with hip rotation. This should unbalance him and knock him off his feet; you will fall on top of him. This throw can be preceded by striking the attacker's knee on the outside with your own knee, or by "in and out." The "in and out" means to strike his opposite leg on the outside with your knee, so that your foot is actually on the inside of his leg and in front of it, next to his ankle, with your shins crossing. Because of the likelihood that you'll fall with him, this isn't an ideal throw for our purposes.

THE CHIP

After you have established your grip, strike the opponent's ankle on the outside, while swinging him in the direction of whichever foot you are striking.[4]

----

[4]. These throws are described in Donald Walker's *Defensive Exercises* (1840). Walker was describing the Cumberland and Westmoreland style of backhold wrestling, but it is generally agreed that this style is identical to Scottish backhold wrestling, differing only in the costumes of the competitors and other inessential details.

SHIFTING

The opponent slashes at you from a high stance. Rather than stepping off the line, you simply shift out of distance to avoid his attack. Your lead foot darts back on the ball of the foot in a position similar to the seventh position of the dirk dance. While your body is out of distance, your arms can still reach your opponent, so you catch his knife hand just as it misses you and before it can strike again. Then you step forward and throw the opponent using one of the techniques described previously.

Bone-Breakings

The *Bretha dein checht*, or *Judgments of Diancecht* (translated by D.A. Binchy), contains a list of the seven principal bone-breakings recognized by Old Irish medical lore:

1. The teeth
2. The upper arm (humerus)
3. The forearm (radius and ulna)
4. The thigh (femur)
5. The shin (tibia)
6. The point of the shoulder (collar-bone, clavicle)
7. The point of the heel (heel bones or wrist bone)

The original Old Irish text reads: "*Ata[t] .uii. cnamcoma(i)gh as sruithiu .i. is uaisli fil i nduine .i. combriste cnama is uaisli fil i nduine .i. a fiacail 7 a doid 7 a righ, sliasait, lurga, delg(n)a gualann. l/ lethcnaim a riged no seireth .i. saldelgo.*" Christopher Vermeers of the Cateran Society first identified the importance of this text to Highland fighting arts.

Described below are some counterattacks that target some of the seven bone-breakings. You can follow up any of these with a throw.

Headbutting.

HEADBUTTING

The opponent passes forward and stabs down at you. You deflect the attack with your free hand while headbutting him in the face. This can be a devastating surprise attack, especially because the instinct is to respond by moving the head back, which will cause the victim to be struck in the teeth. Breaking the teeth is the first of the seven principal bone-breakings.[1]

----

1. This passage was based on the advice of a former gang member from Scotland who had often seen the infamous "Glasgow kiss" in action!

Palm strike displacement.

PALM STRIKE DISPLACEMENT

The opponent passes forward and stabs down at you. You move forward while making a palm strike to his face from below, breaking his teeth. The angle of your free arm must displace his attack as it strikes him, so you will have to adjust both your arm and body position depending on your opponent.[2] This counter must be performed with explosive force, knocking the opponent backward. If you are at all hesitant, your opponent can adjust the angle of his attack and stab you.

....

2. This is the author's interpretation of the action depicted on the right side of the *Drawn After the Quicke* woodcut, where the swordsman appears to be executing such a palm strike to prevent the completion of the knife fighter's attack. Although this technique does seem to be effective in practice if performed explosively, other researchers have drawn different conclusions from the same woodcut, including the idea that the swordsman is waving to the knife fighter or that the two are merely playing or posing.

TRAPPING AND CONTROLLING

The opponent passes forward and attacks you by stabbing straight down. You step forward and to your left to get off the line of attack and to his outside. At the same moment, you catch his right wrist with your right hand and his right elbow with your left hand, sinking down into a low version of the dirk dance's fifth position stance, while locking his elbow to increase the pressure. Then you transfer your weight onto your right foot and carry your left foot over to the right and in front of your own right foot. This will cross your legs and increase the pain of the hold. This targets both the upper arm (second bone-breaking) and the forearm (third bone-breaking). Then, if you turn 360 degrees, your opponent will be forced into a prone position on the floor. Section two of the dirk dance has a series of movements that can be interpreted speculatively in this way.[3]

KICKING

Only low kicks are used in most accounts of Gaelic hand-to-hand combat. In this case, the kick is used as a prelude to a throw. Practice any of the throwing techniques but precede the throw with a snapping kick to the opponent's shins (the fifth bone-breaking), just after you have caught his knife hand. Such a kick will resemble the sixth position of the dirk dance. The

---

3. Christopher Thompson and Louie Pastore, *Combative Techniques in the Scottish Dirk Dance*.

BONE-BREAKINGS • 51 •

Trapping and controlling.

fourth dirk dance position can also be used as a kick that scrapes down the entire length of the shin or that targets the heel (the seventh bone-breaking).[4]

PUNCHING

Punches can target any of the bone-breakings, although you should remember that the thigh (the fourth bone-breaking) is in fact the hardest bone to break in the human body.

The opponent may very well attempt to keep you from counterattacking or drawing your weapon by pulling you off balance or gaining control of your knife hand as he attacks. For example, he may grab the wrist of your knife hand and pull you forcibly toward him, stabbing down at the same moment. In this case, you should deflect with your free hand while sinking the wrist of your knife hand as low as possible. At the same time, step into his attack, bringing your left foot behind his right, and throw him using the crook or back heel. The key is not merely to attempt to resist him as he pulls you forward, but to go with him and turn this momentum to your advantage.[5]

---

4. A number of the dirk dance steps could be interpreted as low kicking attacks, according to Cateran Society researcher Louie Pastore, who has made a detailed study of the dance from the instruction of students of the Fletts. According to Pastore's Web site, "The version of the Dirk Dance taught by Louie Pastore was recovered in Canada by renowned dance researchers Tom and Joan Flett, back in the 1950s. The dance was passed to the Fletts from Mary Isdale McNab, who stipulated that he learn it only on the condition that he would teach it only to a relation, or favorite pupil. Before his death, Mr. Flett only taught John Wesencraft, who agreed to teach Louie the dance in late 2003–04."

5. This is an adaptation of Lesson XXIII of the Highland Officer's *Anti-Pugilism* text.

Knife Against Knife

In some cases, a man with good quickdraw skills could actually get his own weapon into action in time, leading to the rare combat of dirk against dirk.

> His son, while out hunting one day, met the young laird of Lamond travelling with a servant from Cowal towards Inverlochy. They dined together at a house on the Blackmount, between Tyndrum and King's House, but having unfortunately quarrelled during the evening, dirks were drawn, and the young Macgregor was killed.[1]

For the most part, however, a sudden attack left no time to draw one's own weapon. Combat involving dirk against dirk generally occurred only by mutual agreement.

---

1. MacGregor clan history, electricscotland.com/webclans/m/macgreg2.html.

Wagers were freely engaged in, and out of one of these wagers there arose a quarrel between two of the brothers. Like the dogs, they were determined to fight it out, and agreed to settle the dispute at the point of the dirk.

The rest of the brothers, unwilling that any such affair should disgrace their family, strove their utmost to separate the two combatants; but, instead of quelling the dispute, they only succeeded in adding fuel to the fire.

Without further ado lots were cast, and a general and equal-sided fight then began. Fierce and bloody was the fray, and melancholy the result; for not a single man of the brothers remained alive at the end of it, except the youngest, who had taken no active part in the combat.[2]

Dirk combat is particularly dangerous, because the dirk is almost exclusively an offensive weapon. It generally cannot be used to parry despite its length, because there is no guard to protect the hand. Therefore you will have to slip the enemy's attacks with footwork and make extensive use of your free hand in the offensive, defensive, and counteroffensive. If you are close enough to strike the enemy, there is a very high possibility that you will also be struck. As it says in Burt's "Letters": "[I]n a close encounter there is no defense against it." While this is not quite true, the fact remains that the odds of injury in any knife fight are very high, even if you are victorious. Your safety will depend largely on your mastery of distance.

Take note that it is particularly difficult to assess the range of an attacker in the low guards.

Let us assume you have slipped the initial attack and succeeded in drawing your own weapon. This is actually the least likely scenario—in most Gaelic accounts of attacks with the dirk in the oral tradition, the victim does not have the opportunity to draw his own knife.

---

2. "Legends and Traditions: The Craig Liath Mhor," electricscotland.com/kids/stories/liath_mhor.htm.

KNIFE AGAINST KNIFE

Once your weapon is in play, there is a simple strategy that you can follow to defeat your opponent:

ON THE DEFENSIVE

1. Slip the attack with footwork and displace it with your free hand.
2. Counterattack at the same moment you slip the attack.
3. Recover to a guard position or close in and throw the opponent.

ON THE OFFENSIVE

1. Displace any counterattack with your free hand.
2. At the same moment, attack by slashing or stabbing.
3. Recover to a guard position or close in and throw the opponent.

The first two steps actually happen simultaneously or nearly so, followed immediately by the third step. You slip the opponent's attack as you get out of distance and off the line of the attack using your footwork, and you displace the attack as you use your free hand to deflect it away from your body. At the same moment, you must counterattack. As soon as you have completed your counterattack, you either recover immediately to an on-guard position or close in and throw the opponent using one of the throws described herein.

For example, the attacker steps forward and stabs straight down from the first guard. You shift to get out of distance, causing him to miss you. At the same time, you throw your free hand up to your inside high to deflect the attack in case you misjudged the distance. As his attack passes harmlessly by, you cut him in the head from the fourth guard. Seeing that he is cut, you close in and get a grip on his knife hand with your free hand. You put your heel behind his and use the back heel to throw your wounded opponent to the ground. Note that the counterattack

Throwing a wounded opponent.

must come like lightning, at the exact moment that you slip his attack. Also, do not close in for the throw unless you're sure you can get complete control. Recover immediately to a guard position if you are at all unsure.

On the offensive, you use a very similar strategy. Displace any attempted counterattack by using your free hand. At the same moment, close in and cut or stab your opponent. As soon as you have completed your attack, recover to a guard position or close in and throw him.

Going on the Offensive

The first point of this simple strategy of taking the fight to your opponent is to use your free hand to displace any attempted counterattack.

DISPLACING COUNTERATTACKS USING THE FREE HAND

The free hand is used extensively on the offensive. One of the most useful and common free-hand attacks is simply to move in with your free hand at an angle that will suppress an attempted counter. This will depend once again on an understanding of the four zones. Determine where the opponent could possibly strike you if he attacks from his current position, and move in with your free hand ready to displace that attack. Any counter will be deflected, or it will strike your free arm and not the vital targets on your body or head.

It is important to hold your free arm so that the outside of the forearm is facing the opponent, not the vulnerable inner arm. You must keep your free hand open and flexible, ready to take any opportunity to seize control of the opponent's weapon arm.

• 58 • HIGHLAND KNIFE FIGHTING

Pushing the blade aside with the free hand.

The following are some other attacks using the free hand.
1. If you are close enough to each other, push his blade aside with your free hand while attacking him with your dirk. This entire process must be done quickly and smoothly to keep him from cutting your hand or disengaging his weapon.
2. Grab his wrist with your free hand and pull him toward you forcibly, while attacking him with your dirk. You may be able to do this so as to trap his entire weapon arm beneath your free arm. Be careful that he doesn't

Grabbing an opponent's wrist.

step forward and put his left leg behind your right leg to throw you.[1]
3. Grab the wrist of his free hand, especially if he is holding it in front of his body, and pull him toward you forcibly while passing to that side of his body at an angle. This will make it very difficult for him to counter or slip the attack, and his entire left side will be exposed, from his temple to his hamstring. Be careful, however, as he may be holding

---

1. This is also derived from the Highland Officer's *Lesson XXIII*.

Pulling an opponent forcibly toward you.

his arm in front of himself as an invitation, hoping to draw you forward and in range of a counter.[2]

4. Step in while making a palm strike to his face from below, breaking his teeth and driving his jaw up to expose his throat to an attack. If he is in a high position, the angle of your free arm can also prevent his

2. Such an attack appears to be shown in an ancient Scottish carving from Glamis Manse of two warriors fighting with axes, which can be seen on page 22 of Paul Wagner's *Pictish Warrior A.D. 297–841* from Osprey Publishing. It is also found in modern knife fighting, as described by MacYoung in *Knives, Knife Fighting, and Related Hassles*, page 58.

counter, as you move forward and complete the attack.[3] Remember that this must be done with explosive force, or he may stab you under your arm.
5. In close distance, use the free hand to strike the opponent or to assist with grappling.

Remember that any specific technique is likely to occur only rarely in loose play or actual combat. The point of understanding these techniques is not simply to memorize them and apply them when needed; it is also to gain an understanding of the underlying concepts, to be applied with flexibility as the situation requires. With practice, it is possible to become very skillful at displacing attacks and preventing counters with your free hand, even if the specific techniques described here are rarely applied except in drills.

In general, it is much easier to displace an attack or a counter than actually to gain complete control of an opponent's weapon arm. It is much safer to make an attack of your own if you use such a displacement first. As you only need to gain a moment's time to stab or slash your enemy, you can often suppress his counter with a very simple movement of your free hand, followed immediately by your own attack. This does not provide complete protection, but in a knife fight complete protection is often impossible.

In Renaissance German and Italian fighting traditions using similar long-bladed knives, a number of complex trapping techniques are used. While it would be possible to perform such techniques with the dirk, they do not seem to have been as common in the British Isles, as evidenced by the words of George Silver.

First know that to this weapon there belongeth no Wards nor grips but against such a one as is foolehardy and will suf-

---

3. This is my interpretation of the action depicted on the right side of the *Drawn After the Quicke* woodcut.

fer himself to have a full stabb in the face or bodye to hazard the giving of Another, then against him you may use your left hand in throwinge him aside or strike up his heels after you have stabbed him.

Silver advises the dagger fighter to stay out of distance, slip his opponent's attacks with "continual motion," and strike the opponent the instant he comes within distance.[4]

Much of Silver's philosophy can be seen readily in the Highland fencing manuals, so it seems likely that Highland fighters followed a similar approach and avoided the complex trapping techniques found in Germany and Italy.

THE ATTACK

The dirk can be used to attack the opponent by slashing or stabbing. From the first guard, you can stab downward forcibly at any target or slash by turning the wrist as you attack.

The second guard is especially good for slashing attacks. From this position a slash can bring you up into a first or third guard, from which you can stab immediately. It can be difficult to avoid an attack from the low guards, because it is hard to see the angle of the attack. However, slashes are most effective against unprotected areas of the body, such as exposed flesh or areas covered only by light clothing.

The belted plaid worn by the old Highlanders would have been effective light armor against the slash. At the time, many people in Europe wore layers of thick clothing as protection against the elements. In these situations, a stab would prove more effective. Highlanders were known for wearing little protection against the cold, so slashing attacks may have been more effective among them than in some other areas of Europe at that time.

....

4. Paul Wagner, *Master of Defence: The Works of George Silver* (Paladin Press 2003): 313.

GOING ON THE OFFENSIVE

From the fourth guard, you can make a very powerful cut, or you can stab by extending your arm.

THE FEINT

The feint can be particularly useful with the dirk, since the dirk can be moved much more rapidly than the sword. Therefore, it is more feasible while wielding the dirk to use multiple feints to confuse and unnerve the opponent before you launch a committed attack.

THE INVITATION

As with the sword, you can deliberately leave an opening to tempt your enemy into attacking that opening. As you can predict where your enemy is going to attack, you can plan your counter accordingly.

THE CONTINUATION

A continued attack is an attack made after a pass or a step in, without recovering. The continuation can leave you exposed, often making it too dangerous to attempt, but it can be a useful tactic in conjunction with using the free hand. For example, you can deflect the opponent's weapon in close distance and then slash your dirk across his Adam's apple, which will leave your dirk in the third guard. If he slips this attack, you can stab at his sternum immediately from that position.

THE RECOVERY OR THROWING OF THE OPPONENT

There are two ways to recover from an attack. The first way is simply to draw your front leg back to an on-guard position, either by executing a reverse pass or simply pulling the lead foot back. In other words, your body will be in the same position as at the start of a fight. You would use this type of recovery if the opponent slips your attack but does not follow up with an attack of his own.

If the opponent does attempt an attack, you can recover into a shift, or you can traverse off the line of the attack, thus slipping his attack and giving you the opportunity to counter.

Your other option at this range is to throw the opponent. Because your dirk is still in your hand, you won't be able to use your knife hand to get a grip. Instead, use the false (unsharpened) edge of the dirk as a lever, hooking it behind the opponent's neck or shoulder as you go for the throw. (This is shown in the first section of the dirk dance.)[5]

---

5. Thompson and Pastore, *Combative Techniques in the Scottish Dirk Dance*.

The Dirk Dance Positions

In close distance, you will make use of the eight dirk dance positions.

- **First position:** This can be used to backsweep an opponent's legs in close distance.[1]
- **Second position:** This can be used as a trip, or as a low kick.[2]
- **Third position:** This can be used to avoid a leg sweep, or it can be used as a knee block or a leg trap, wrapping your leg behind the opponent's knee and locking your foot behind the leg.[3]
- **Fourth position:** This can be used to sweep the back of the opponent's knee using your heel, to strike with the knee, or to kick the thigh. The "double touch" and "hanking" in traditional wrestling also resemble this movement.[4]

....

1. This is the Fletts' "4th rear int aerial" position.
2. This is the Fletts' "4th int aerial" position.
3. This is the Fletts' "rear leg" position.
4. This is the Fletts' "front leg" position.

- **Fifth position:** This resembles a higher version of the horse stance of Eastern martial arts (although it would probably have been performed lower by the old-style dancers than it is today). It can be used as part of a trapping and controlling counter when your own weapon is not available, as previously described in the section on unarmed defense.[5]
- **Sixth position:** This can be used as a low, probing sideways kick or as a sweep.[6]
- **Seventh position:** This somewhat resembles the cat stance of Eastern martial arts or the shift of broadsword fencing. It can be used to stand on and trap an opponent's foot or to stomp on a prone opponent.[7]
- **Eighth position:** This can be used as a sweeping kick that shoots out suddenly in close distance.[8]

For instruction in the traditional Scottish dirk dance, contact Louie Pastore of Greenock, Scotland (http://dirkdance.tripod.com).

There are many ways to apply this footwork in combat. For example, you can close the distance, immobilize his weapon arm with your free hand, hook your dirk behind his neck, and use your right foot in the fourth position to strike the knee of his lead leg, using the dirk to drag him over and down to your left.

From the fourth guard, you can pass forward and make a horizontal cut at the opponent's throat, immediately followed by backsweeping his right leg with your left leg in the first position. If you hold the dirk in front of the body, you can close the distance while using a low, probing kick or sweep in the sixth position, and then use the fourth position to avoid any attempted sweep or leg strike or to kick his shin with your heel.[9]

---

5. This is the Fletts' "2nd" position.
6. This is the Fletts' "2nd aerial" position.
7. This is the Fletts' "5th" position.
8. This is the Fletts' "4th aerial" position.
9. Thompson and Pastore, *Combative Techniques in the Scottish Dirk Dance.*

THE DIRK DANCE POSITIONS

FOOT POSITIONS OF THE DIRK DANCE
Illustrated by Louie Pastore
In each case, the black-shoed figure is the one performing the technique.

You can use any of the throws or bone-breakings described in the section on unarmed defense. It is possible that you'll end up in a situation where you have caught your opponent's knife hand and he has also caught yours, a scenario in which both of you are attempting to get a throw. In this case, some of these techniques may be used against you.

If the opponent has you in the lock, keep your weight forward to keep him from throwing you backward, while being careful that he does not throw you forward either.

To prevent the opponent from throwing you with the buttock or cross buttock, you can take the lock from behind your opponent, while pulling your head down to slip through his grip. You can also resist the cross buttock by loosening your hold, with your weight forward and your feet firm on the ground. If you are much faster than your opponent, you can sometimes use the back heel on him as he begins this throw.

To prevent the swinging hipe, lower your breast against the opponent as he tries to lift you, so as to trap the opponent's right arm in place with your left arm, near the elbow. Meet his strike against your left knee with your own right knee. If he fails to lift you, you will have improved your hold.[10]

If the opponent tries to headbutt you, do not move the head back, which will cause you to be struck in the teeth. A better response is to move to the side, to move the entire body back, to move the head into the attack rather than away from it (striking the attacker in the nose), or to strike the attacker's face with your elbow.[11]

The punch can be used against a variety of targets, and punching to the small of the back can prevent some throws.

The elbow can be used to strike the chest during a throw. You can break out of an opponent's hold by digging your elbow into

---

10. Walker, *Defensive Exercises*.
11. Based on the advice of a former gang member and streetfighter from Scotland.

the hollow of his elbow to break his grip. An elbow to the chin or chest can prevent an attack in close distance.[12]

In a worst-case scenario where a stronger opponent is overpowering you on the ground, you can do as Cameron of Lochiel did to Colonel Pellew and bite out his throat.

In close distance, the danger of a mutual hit is extremely high. A common close distance situation would be an assassination, which historically would have occurred if one were seeking revenge, especially as part of a blood feud. In this scenario, your opponent should not have his weapon drawn when you attack. You would rely on stealth, deception, and your quickdraw skills.

---

12. Ken Pfrenger, "Celtic Wrestling" (unpublished article).

Exercises and Drills

STABBING AND SLASHING EXERCISES

You should practice stabbing and slashing from the guards at a variety of angles and targets. Combine this with the footwork you have already been practicing, including advancing, retreating, shifting, traversing, leaping, passing, stepping in, and so forth. The shift and the step in will be especially useful. As the dirk was often used in close quarters against multiple opponents, you should practice stabbing and slashing while wheeling from side to side, turning to face enemies from every direction, and stabbing and slashing at opponents in front of you, behind you, and to either side.

Whether stabbing or slashing, the movement of the dirk must begin the attack just before you step forward, so that the dirk is in front of you as you attack. This should be performed as one continuous motion.

TWELVE DOORS OF THE SOUL EXERCISE

Old Irish medical lore included a curious list of the so-called Twelve Doors of the Soul, preserved in a text called the *Bretha dein checht* (*Judgments of Diancecht*), translated by D.A. Binchy. These were the 12 places on a human body where injuries were most likely to be fatal, according to medieval Irish healers.

Christopher Vermeers of the Cateran Society suggests that this knowledge might have been widespread among Gaelic warriors, as it would have been useful to them to know where best to aim their attacks. Such combative anatomies are found in other martial arts around the world, including Japanese kenjutsu.

Further research confirms that this list is entirely accurate medically, and that Gaelic lore contains a number of references to warriors attacking these particular targets (or trying to protect these targets from being attacked). We do not know whether Scots Gaelic warriors categorized such knowledge into the Twelve Doors as the *Bretha dein checht* does, but they do seem to have been aware that injuries to these areas were especially dangerous. Therefore, the Twelve Doors of the Soul are important in Cateran Society training. The Twelve Doors are as follows:

1. The crown of the head
2. The hollow of the occiput
3. The hollow of the temple (temporal fossa)
4. The apple of the throat (Adam's apple)
5. The hollow of the breast (cavity of the throat)
6. The armpit
7. The breastbone (sternum)
8. The navel (umbilicus)
9. The bend of the elbow (antecubital fossa)
10. The hollow of the ham (hamstring, or crook of the hough)
11. The bulge of the groin (femoral triangle)
12. The sole of the foot

A few of these targets would not necessarily be easy to reach in combat. The hollow of the occiput (door two), although a very vulnerable spot, could not easily be struck except from behind, although there are occasions in which this door can be attacked during in-fighting or in an assassination.

The sole of the foot would rarely be a target, although it is vulnerable to arrow strikes. Attacks to a certain spot on the foot were used by Japan's Kashima Shinryu tradition for assassinations, but it is possible that the primary danger to this door is not from combat but from tetanus caused by stepping on infected objects.

This leaves ten doors that are viable targets in a typical fight. I have retained the original numbering of the doors for the sake of consistency, although in most exercises we'll skip over doors two and twelve.

For now, all you need to know is that our attacks will be focused on these targets whenever possible. (In loose play, some of the doors may have to be avoided for reasons of safety, as an injury to these areas could prove too dangerous even with safety gear.)

When performing this exercise, remember to stab and slash correctly, with the dirk preceding any body movement but striking the target at the same moment you complete your step. Vary your practice, sometimes including an initial motion of taking control of the enemy's weapon arm or free hand with your free hand. Combine the attacks with a variety of footwork, including stepping in, passing forward, and striking from immobility. This exercise is performed solo, facing a dummy, a chart of the Twelve Doors, or a person standing well out of distance.

The Twelve Doors Exercise
1. Take the first guard. Stab the crown of the head (door one) and recover.
2. Stab the temple (door three), recover to the first guard, and lower your dirk into the second guard.
3. Slash diagonally upward across the Adam's apple (door four), finishing in the third guard.
4. From that position, stab the hollow of the breast (door five) and recover to the fifth guard.
5. Stab the armpit (door six) and recover to the fifth guard.

6. Stab the sternum (door seven) and recover to the fifth guard.
7. Stab the navel (door eight) and recover to the fourth guard.
8. Slash downward, turning the wrist, against the bend of the elbow (door nine), recovering to the fourth guard.
9. Slash across the hamstring of the opponent's forward leg (door ten) and recover while changing to the second guard.
10. Slash upward into the opponent's groin (door eleven) and recover to the first guard.

THE "LESLIE" EXERCISE

This is an advanced loose play exercise using safe practice dirks. It is modeled after a celebrated incident in a feud between the Leslies and the Leiths. The students are placed in random locations in an enclosed area. One of them is secretly chosen to be the attacker. All will have their weapons sheathed. At a prearranged signal, the chosen student will draw his dirk and attempt to leave the enclosed area while stabbing or slashing as many students as possible along the way. None of the others may draw their weapons until the first attack has been made, but once this has occurred, they may do their best to strike or evade the attacker.

This exercise trains all the students in a common historical scenario with the dirk—a surprise attack carried out as part of a blood feud.[1]

TWO-PERSON DRILLS

Drill 1

Defender: Take the first guard.

Antagonist: Take the first guard and attack by stabbing straight down.

---

[1] The incident of "Leslie Amo' the Leiths" is described by Logan in *Scottish Gael*.

EXERCISES AND DRILLS • 75 •

Deflect the attack and stab the hollow of the breast.

Defender: Step in as he attacks while deflecting his attack with your free hand. As you do this, stab the hollow of the breast. You should practice this scenario with several variations: with a simple deflection, with a wrist grab (with the hand turned so the thumb is on the opposite side of his wrist), and with a palm strike to his face from below, driving his jaw up to expose his throat to an attack. You will have to adjust the angle of your free arm for each opponent and possibly also crouch down or pass forward obliquely as you counter, so that your free arm will displace his strike. The risk in using the palm strike is that he will redirect and stab your body below the arm, so it must be performed explosively. Although you should develop skill with this palm strike counter, it is much more likely that you would use a simple deflection or possibly a wrist grab in actual combat.[2]

2. This is based on my interpretation of the action depicted on the right side of the *Drawn After the Quicke* woodcut.

Drill 2

Defender: Take the second guard.

Antagonist: Take the second guard. Attack by slashing straight up, bringing your dirk into the first guard.

Defender: Slip the attack and then begin to move in toward the opponent.

Antagonist: When your initial attack is slipped, attack again by stabbing straight down.

Defender: Deflect the attack with your free hand. As you do this, slash across his Adam's apple, bringing your dirk into the third guard.

Antagonist: Slip the attack to your throat.

Defender: From the third guard, stab him in the hollow of the breast as you continue to move forward.

EXERCISES AND DRILLS

Shift to avoid the attack.

Deflect the attack and slash the throat.

The opponent avoids your slash.

EXERCISES AND DRILLS

Continue forward and stab the throat, using your free hand to suppress any counter.

Drill 3

Defender: Take the first guard.

Antagonist: Take the second guard. Attack by slashing horizontally, bringing your dirk into the third guard.

Defender: Slip the attack, then move toward the opponent while preparing to displace with your free hand.

Antagonist: From the third guard, stab at his sternum.

Defender: Displace the attack with your left hand, gaining control of his weapon arm if you can. As you do this, continue to move forward and stab down at the hollow of the breast or the sternum.

EXERCISES AND DRILLS • 81 •

Avoid the attack by shifting.

Displace his second attack . . .

EXERCISES AND DRILLS

... *and move in with a stab.*

Drill 4

Defender: Take the first guard.

Antagonist: Take the first guard and attack with a downward stab.

Defender: Displace the attack with your free hand. As you do this, stab downward at his sternum.

EXERCISES AND DRILLS • 85 •

Displace the attack with your free hand and counter to the sternum.

Drill 5

Take a position in which both fighters have attacked from the first guard with a downward stab and both have caught their opponent's wrist, resulting in a stalemate.

Defender: Put your left foot behind the opponent's right leg and pull it toward you, while pushing his free arm away from you with your weapon arm, throwing him to the ground.[3]

---

3. This drill introduces a throw from Highland wrestling.

EXERCISES AND DRILLS • 87 •

Stalemate.

Break the stalemate immediately by throwing the opponent.

Drill 6

Defender: Stand in the fourth guard.

Antagonist: Stand in the fifth guard. Thrust at the defender.

Defender: Slip the attack by shuffling back diagonally with your left foot to remove yourself from the line of attack, while simultaneously making cut 1 (diagonally descending from your right). (The directions of cuts are as numbered in broadsword fencing. Refer to the glossary for more information.)

Follow this up immediately by reversing the direction of the blade and making cut 4, ripping the point back up along the same line by which it descended. Finish with a sweep, throwing your wounded opponent to the ground.

The opponent thrusts from the fifth guard.

Avoid the attack while cutting the opponent.

Make a second cut along the same line.

Assassination Drill

You should practice assassination skills with the dirk—not because you will ever have any occasion to use them, but because this was a common historical use of the weapon.

One trick is to approach your opponent with your weapon drawn but concealed. In the typical reverse position used by the Highlanders, the dirk can easily be held up against the arm so as to be invisible. In the forward grip, the dirk can be concealed by folding your arms as people typically do in conversation.[4] Experiment with this and other methods of getting close to an enemy with your dirk already drawn. When you launch the attack, don't just stab or slash. You should also suppress any attempted counter through body positioning, displacement, seizing control of his weapon hand, pulling him off balance sharply, or some other means.

The victim in this exercise should practice the skills described in this book—getting out of distance and off line, drawing his own weapon while using his free hand to displace the attack. He should also practice other methods of dealing with a surprise attack, such as moving in as the attack begins and using one of the throws or bone-breakings. Ideally, this could be carried out as an actual surprise attack drill—for example, you could announce at the beginning of a practice session that you will be "assassinating" the students with a safe training weapon at random points during the lesson. This will help teach them to spot the small signs of an approaching attack and to respond appropriately.

In reality, a person attacked by surprise with a dirk will almost never have time to draw his own weapon. Realistically, he must respond as if unarmed, or he will probably be killed. Therefore, if your training partner manages to draw his dirk, you have not carried out an effective attack.

....

4. MacYoung, *Knives, Knife Fighting and Related Hassles*, pp. 43–53 and 71–72.

Drill 7

Defender: Stand in the fourth guard.
Antagonist: Stand in the fifth guard. Thrust at the defender.
Defender: Slip the attack by shuffling back diagonally with your left foot so as to remove yourself from the line of attack, while simultaneously making cut 2 (diagonally descending from your left). Follow this up immediately by reversing the direction of the blade and making cut 3, ripping the point back up along the same line by which it descended. Finish with a sweep, throwing your wounded opponent to the ground.

ADVANCED QUICKDRAW DRILL

Do not think of this drill as a realistic scenario. If you were attacked simultaneously from the front and behind, you would almost certainly be struck. Rather, this is an opportunity to improve your evasion and quickdraw skills by practicing an extremely difficult slip, draw, and counter with safe training weapons.

Defender: Begin with your dirk sheathed and your arms at your side.
Antagonist 1: Begin with your dirk sheathed and your arms at your side, facing the defender. Draw the dirk and attack with a downward stab.
Antagonist 2: Begin with your dirk sheathed and your arms at your side, behind the defender. Draw the dirk and attack with a downward stab.
Defender: Displace the attack from the front with your free hand. As you do this, draw the dirk, stepping backward and off the line of attack with your rear foot. As you do this, stab behind you immediately at antagonist 2. From this position, turn back toward antagonist 1 while slashing across his Adam's apple.

EXERCISES AND DRILLS • 93 •

Advanced quickdraw drill 1, 2, and 3.

Combative Techniques in the Scottish Dirk Dance

by Christopher Thompson
and Louie Pastore

Louie Pastore is the head of the Cateran Society's branch in Scotland. He has extensive experience in the interpretation of the kata of Asian martial arts. He teaches the dirk dance at his academy in Scotland.

It is not surprising that dancing was one of the exercises taught at the Highland martial arts schools, since several dances are known to have been combative in nature. These dances could have been used to train the common clansmen in the rudiments of swordplay.

There was a dance that demonstrated combat with the broadsword and targe, or perhaps with the dirk and targe. This battle dance, which may have been called the *Bruicheath*, was still practiced by traditional Highland dancers in the 19th century. According to James Logan, author of *The Scottish Gael*, two brothers named MacLennan performed this dance in London in 1850. One of them taught it to his grandnephew William MacLennan, the last person known to have been proficient at the *Bruicheath*. He taught the dance to his younger brother, D.G. MacLennan, who illustrated it in his *Highland and Traditional Scottish Dances* in 1950. However, the younger MacLennan no longer remembered how to perform the dance. MacLennan recalls:

The Dirk Dance was a remarkable relic of the Gael, but, with the change of times and customs, few Highlanders now have the least knowledge of it. It was called in Gaelic "Bruicheath," or Battle Dance, and it was a form of "dueling" dance—attack and defence. It may have originated after the style of similar fighting dances in other lands, but it was practiced in the Highlands for centuries. The antagonists carried a dirk in the right hand and shield, or targe, on the left arm, and, facing each other, went through a series of movements representing a combat, alternating this with lightfooted and agile dancing steps.

In Logan's "Scottish Gael" (revised edition 1876, Vol. 1,) it is mentioned that "the Dirk Dance was last performed in London in 1850 by two brothers of the name of MacLennan, who were almost the only individuals who could execute it." ... These MacLennans above referred to were granduncles of mine, and from one of them, my eldest brother, the late William MacLennan, learned the dance. We used to practice it with singlestick, instead of dangerous dirks, but William, being the Scottish champion fencer with sword and cutlass, usually gave me (a youth) a "drubbing."[1]

From the descriptions given by MacLennan, it appears that the movements in this dance were not entirely predetermined. This dance seems to have been a restricted form of loose play, performed to bagpipe music and with dance steps. The goal may have been to "break the head" (draw blood above the eyebrows) as in English singlestick. This seems especially likely, in view of the fact that another old combat dance from Skye (now lost) was called *"Buailidh mi thu 's d' cheann"* ("I will strike you in the head").[2]

....

1. D.G. MacLennan, *Highland and Traditional Scottish Dances*, 1950, p. 32.
2. MacLennan, *Highland and Traditional Scottish Dances*, p. 86.

Such a combination of dance and combat is found in other martial arts of the world, such as Brazilian capoeira and Indonesian penjak silat.

MacLennan called his dance the *Bruicheath* (a word of uncertain meaning), or dirk dance, but as targes and singlesticks were used, the intended weapon may in fact have been the broadsword rather than the dirk. Perhaps the dirk was sometimes used as a substitute for the sword.

In any case, other dirk dances are mentioned in a number of sources, and some of these are fighting dances between two people, in which one is slain and then resuscitated with ritual overtones.[3]

However, only one Scottish dirk dance is still known to this day. This is the dance taught by Mary Isdale McNab to J.F. and T.M. Flett. McNab learned the dance from D.C. Mather, who (according to the Fletts) may have learned it while observing the MacLennan brothers in 1892. At this time William was arranging a solo version of the dance that was not being danced anywhere, so it is possible Mr. Mather could have created his own version from this. On the other hand, Mather had an extensive knowledge of how Highland dancing was taught in the Highland regiments, learning to dance and play the pipes at a school for orphans of families of Scottish regiments. He later entered the service of Lieutenant Colonel MacDougall of Lunga and took prizes for dancing at various Highland games.

In his dance, the dirk is held point up like a sword, although in comb the dirk is usually held point down. This may also be an indication that this dance was originally performed with a sword.

In the Indonesian silat tradition, dances are frequently catalogs of combative techniques, much like the kata of Japanese martial arts. When these dances are compared with ancient wrestling methods, they are found to contain the same movements and principles. We know that such a connection was also

....

3. Flett, *Traditional Step-Dancing in Scotland*, p. 45.

made in Gaelic culture, for the old Highland *taigh suntais* (martial training academies) and Highland regiments in the British Army also taught the arts of dancing as well as war.

Unfortunately, we do not know for certain that the Fletts' dirk dance is derived from the *Bruicheath* of the MacLennans, or that alterations were not made for aesthetic reasons at some point in the dance's history, thus diluting its combative nature. Therefore, our analysis of martial techniques in the dirk dance is inherently speculative. However, close examination of the dance does seem to reveal a number of specific fighting techniques.

You should keep in mind that the older style of Highland dance used lower stances and heavier footwork than is common today, and in martial terms the movements discussed here should be based on that older style. However, the best way to learn how to use these methods effectively would be to combine a study of Highland dance with traditional Scottish loosehold or backhold wrestling and more typical martial arts training. To learn the dirk dance itself, you could either study it directly from someone who knows the dance or learn it from the Fletts' book, *Traditional Step-Dancing in Scotland,* after you have studied Highland dance. This would provide a much clearer picture of the footwork and its potential martial applications than can be gleaned from an essay such as this one.

Highland dancers have a terminology of their own for the various steps used in their style. The Fletts added a number of modifications to this to describe the wider array of positions in the older dances described by their informants. Because the dirk dance uses only a small selection of these, I have renamed the positions to make them easier to learn. The foot positions found in the dirk dance are (in the order in which they appear in the dance) as follows:

- **First Position:** This is the Fletts' "4th rear int aerial" position. It can be used to backsweep an opponent's legs in close distance and is similar to the sweep shown in tafel 211 of Talhoffer's Fechtbuch of 1467.

- **Second Position:** This is the Fletts' "4th int aerial" position. It can be used like the trippet of traditional wrestling or as a low kick. A similar kicking movement is shown in Petter's Ring-Buch, part 4 number 4.
- **Third Position:** This is the Fletts' "rear leg" position. It can be used to avoid a leg sweep, or it can be used as a knee block or a leg trap, wrapping your leg behind the opponent's knee and locking your foot behind your leg. Petter's Ring-Buch shows a similar movement in part 3 number 1.
- **Fourth Position:** This is the Fletts' "front leg" position. It can be used to sweep the back of the opponent's knee using your heel, to strike with the knee as in Petter's Ring-Buch part 3 number 7, and to kick the thigh as in Talhoffer's Fechtbuch tafel 210. The "double touch" and "hanking" in traditional wrestling are also similar to this movement.
- **Fifth Position:** This is the Fletts' "2nd" position. It resembles a higher version of the horse stance of Eastern martial arts (although it would probably have been performed lower by the old-style dancers than it is today). It can be used as part of a trapping and controlling counter when your own weapon is not available. For example, if an opponent attacks you with a dirk and you do not have time to draw your own weapon, you can catch his right wrist with your right hand and his right elbow with your left hand, sinking into this fifth position stance while locking his elbow to increase the pressure. Then you would transfer your weight onto your right foot and carry your left foot over to the right and in front of your own right foot. This will cross your legs and increase the pain of the hold. Then, if you turn 360 degrees, your opponent will be forced into a prone position on the floor. Part of a similar technique can be seen in Petter's *Ring-Buch*, part 6 number 2. Section 2 of the dirk dance includes a

series of motions that can be interpreted speculatively in this way.
- **Sixth Position:** This is the Fletts' "2nd aerial" position. It can be used as a low, probing sideways kick or as a sweep, and is similar to Petter's Ring-Buch, part 11 number 8.
- **Seventh Position:** This is the Fletts' 5th position. It somewhat resembles the cat stance of Eastern martial arts or the shift of broadsword fencing. It can be used to stand on and trap an opponent's foot or to stomp on a prone opponent, as in the scenario described above under the fifth position.
- **Eighth Position:** This is the Fletts' "4th aerial" position. It can be used as a sweeping kick that shoots out suddenly in close distance, as in Petter's Ring-Buch, part 7 number 3.

The footwork described here is used in a number of combinations in the dance itself, providing a catalog of potential techniques that can be used in any sequence and have many possible applications.

In the dance, the dirk is generally held over the head in the same position as the St. George guard of regimental broadsword play. In other words, it is used as a short sword, which is possible only because the dirk is an extraordinarily long knife, as long as 20 inches overall. These methods would not be nearly as feasible with a shorter knife, and it is possible that a broadsword may originally have been the intended weapon in the dance.

From this guard, you can pass forward and make a horizontal cut 5 at the opponent's throat, immediately followed by back-sweeping his right leg with your left leg in the first position. The dirk dance opens with a set of motions similar to this.

If you wish to throw your opponent rather than immediately kill him, you can close the distance, hook your dirk behind his neck, and use your right foot in the fourth position to strike the knee of his lead leg, and then use the dirk to drag him over and down to your left. The first section of the dirk dance also includes a series of actions that can be interpreted in this way; although to perform the technique safely, you would need to immobilize his weapon arm.

If you are in the fourth guard and an opponent thrusts at you with his weapon, you can slip the attack by shuffling back diagonally with your left foot to remove yourself from the line of attack, while simultaneously making cut 1 (diagonally descending from your right). You can follow this up immediately by reversing the direction of the blade and making cut 4, ripping the point back up along the same line by which it descended. You can then finish with a sweep, with your right foot in the second position, throwing your wounded opponent to the ground. This sequence appears to be shown in the third section of the dirk dance. An alternate version is also included, in which you initially make cut 2 and then come back up with cut 3.

Section three of the dance also includes a section in which the dirk is held at shoulder level, in a position similar to the open guard of the older styles of swordplay—again reinforcing the possibility that a sword was originally intended here. From this stance, if the opponent cuts at you, you can sidestep to the right to move out of the line of attack. Pivoting full circle while remaining close to your attacker, you can cut him horizontally across his stomach with cut 5 or 6 and then unbalance him with a low kick in the second position as you rip the point up from his stomach to his throat.

In section four of the dance, the dirk is held in front of the body in the same position as the medium guard of the older style of swordplay. From this position you can close the distance while using a low, probing kick or sweep in the sixth position, and then use the fourth position to avoid his attempted sweep or leg strike or to kick his shin with your heel.

The fourth section of the dance also includes a remarkable and athletic feat, which is described in Gaelic oral tradition as the "swordsman's leap" and considered an esoteric ability with sinister connotations. In the swordsman's leap as described in the tale of Domhnull og na h-Alba, the warrior leaps high into the air and cuts or thrusts at his opponent from there.[4]

The variation included in the dirk dance is somewhat more complex, as the dancer appears to use this technique to avoid and counter an attack from behind. In this sequence, you are attacked from behind with a low cut to your legs. You leap over the cut (a move still used in French canne fighting) while simultaneously turning in midair to cut your attacker's sword arm.

In section five of the dirk dance, the dancer no longer has the dirk in hand. Both the hands either rest on the dancer's hips or are raised in the air. If this is interpreted as a series of techniques for an unarmed man to defeat an armed attacker, it could show such methods as pulling the opponent in close by his wrists, upper arms, shoulders or neck, while using the footwork above to sweep or kick him to the ground.

In section six, the dirk is picked up again, and the footwork once again may represent sweeps, leg locks, or evasions. Most of section six is a repeat of section three, so it is possible that the missing nine sections of the dance were largely repetitive of the six sections that were taught to the Fletts.

One principle that can be observed repeatedly in these sequences is to wound the opponent with your weapon and then immediately throw him to the ground with wrestling footwork. This would reduce the risk of being slain by a vengeful opponent after you have mortally wounded him.

There has been some question about the antiquity of the dirk dance as taught to the Fletts. James Logan, in *The Scottish Gael*, mentions that an old Gael denied to him that the dirk dance of that time was the same one he had seen in his youth. However, this could mean that the dance he was shown represented a different strand of tradition than the one with which he was familiar. It is also unclear whether D.C. Mather invented the dance

---

4. Smith, *Glenshee*, pp. 79–83.

himself or borrowed it from the MacLennans while making substantial modifications that would have altered the original intent. It is also possible that some parts of the dance were originally intended as interludes with no combative application.

Still, the dance as taught to the Fletts retains several features that suggest it may represent a genuine survival of the martial tradition, even if modified. These include the swordsman's leap, which is confirmed by the story of Domhnull og na h-Alba, and the use of stances corresponding to the St. George, open and medium guards of historical swordplay. These almost certainly would not have been independently known to D.C. Mather, as the fencing stances of his time were quite different. There is also a similarity between how the dance was passed on and how some of the most secretive Asian kata or forms are transmitted. According to the Fletts, Mrs. McNab, who taught them the dance, did so only on the express condition that it was their personal dance, not to be taught to anyone else. After Mrs. MacNab's death in 1966, Tom Flett reluctantly taught the dance to only one other person in his lifetime. Later, after Tom Flett's death, his wife felt it necessary to publish the steps before they were lost forever.

Our analysis of the dance is still in the early stages, and no doubt it will be modified over time. It seems likely, however, that the dirk dance is a living remnant of the Gaelic martial arts tradition and a vital link to the past.

Appendix 2

The Manx Dirk Dance

The Manx Gaels also have a dirk dance, which is performed in a different manner than the Scots Gaelic version. This dance is particularly interesting, in that it has overtly esoteric symbolism drawn from ancient Celtic mythology. However, the dance is controversial, and some scholars consider it a hoax rather than a genuine relic of Manx tradition. According to folklorist Stephen Miller in his introduction to *Mona Davis: Manx Folk-Song, Folk Dance, Folk Lore* (Chiollagh Books, 1994), "The originator of this dance, Jack Kermode, was well known as a joker." He refers to the dance as "an arch piece of fakelore." He provides no evidence for this assertion, however, other than to refer to the dance as a product of misguided romanticism on the part of its collector, Mona Douglas.

As in the Scottish dirk dance, it is possible that the weapon was originally intended to be a sword. In her article "The Manx Dirk Dance as Ritual," Mona Douglas wrote, "The crouch and pick-up after the first dance round the sword is a demonstration of the performer's speed and surety of attack; the kicking of the sword is a test of both the weapon's strength and the dancer's agility; the slashes and changing of the sword from right hand to left show that he can fight on, even if wounded in the sword arm . . ."

The dance was associated with the Manx kings, and in this respect Kermode must have been very knowledgeable about ancient Celtic religious beliefs if he did create the dance as a hoax. The dancer, who is always male, was said to represent the king gaining the blessings of the sun for his people, and before the dance began Kermode was always served a beaker of whiskey in a ceremonial manner by his wife, who then sang the mouth music for the dance. This matches the Celtic mythology of Sovereignty as a goddess who bestows kingship in the form of an intoxicating drink—a remarkable coincidence if Kermode was a trickster as Miller claims. In any case, the Manx dirk dance, whether genuine or not, is still performed from time to time.

The Cateran Society

Appendix 3

F ounded by Christopher Thompson, the Cateran Society is devoted to researching and practicing the historic Gaelic martial arts. If you would like more information about the Cateran Society, including how to join, please check out its Web site at http://www.cateransociety.com.

Glossary

ballock dagger: A medieval style of dagger, considered to be the prototype for the dirk.
***biodag*:** Gaelic for dirk.
cuts: The directions of cuts are numbered in broadsword fencing, as this text refers several times to the numbers of the cuts. Cut 1 is diagonally descending from the right, cut 2 is diagonally descending from the left, cut 3 is diagonally ascending from the right, cut 4 is diagonally ascending from the left, cut 5 is horizontal from the right, cut 6 is horizontal from the left, and cut 7 is a straight cut downwards.
dirk: A long knife, generally sharp on one edge and the top few inches of the other edge. In Gaelic, the dirk is called a *biodag*.
guard, engaging guard: A stance used in combat.
medium guard: A guard used in broadsword fencing. The high medium guard is held with the blade vertical and the point aimed straight upward. The low medium guard is held with the point aimed at the opponent's eyes.
regimental broadsword style: The style of Highland broadsword fencing used in the Scottish Highland regiments.

Scottish backhold: The traditional style of wrestling found at Highland Games. The wrestler takes a hold around his opponent's back and attempts to throw him to the ground using one of several traditional throws.

***sgian*:** Gaelic for a knife of any type. A *sgian achlais* is the small knife worn under the armpit. A *sgian dubh* is a dress knife derived from the *sgian achlais*. In this book, *sgian* is used to refer to a small knife used as a backup weapon to the longer dirk.

targe: The small, round shield or target used by the Highlanders. In Gaelic, it is called a *targaid*.

true edge: The edge that is used for cutting the opponent; the edge that faces out toward the opponent. The other edge is called the false edge. On a dirk, only the true edge and the top of the false edge are sharpened.

About the Authors

Christopher Scott Thompson is the author of two novels, *A Season of Strange Dreams* and *And Then the Night*, both available from BeWrite Books (BeWrite.net). He is also the author of a poetry collection (*City at the Edge of Night*), a new translation of Baudelaire's classic *Flowers of Evil*, and *Lannaireachd: Gaelic Swordsmanship*, a training manual on the use of the Highland broadsword. A resident of Portland, Maine, Thompson is the president of the Cateran Society. Contact the author at one of the following Web sites: www.noctiviganti.com or www.cateransociety.com.

After devoting almost 20 years to the study of Asian martial arts, **Louie Pastore** turned his attention in 2000 to researching martial arts that were practiced throughout Scotland and Europe. In 2004 he was accepted as a pupil of John Wesencraft, the only surviving teacher of the Highland dirk dance as taught to Tom Flett in the 1950s.